AS FAR AS YOU CAN SEE

— Living a Lifestyle —
of Supernatural Faith

Bill Winston

Published by HigherLife Publishing & Marketing, Inc.
PO Box 623307
Oviedo, FL 32762
AHigherLife.com

Cover and Interior Design by Faithe Thomas, Master Design Marketing, LLC
ISBN (Paperback):978-1-954533-55-4
ISBN (Ebook): 978-1-954533-55-4
Library of Congress # 1-10889777571

Printed in the United States of America.

Contents

Introduction

As Far As Your Eye Can See

IN GENESIS, GOD DIRECTED Abraham (who was called Abram at the time) to look around him in every direction and claim the land God was giving him as his own. He wanted Abraham to walk by faith as far as his eyes could see.

> After Lot had gone, the Lord said to Abram, "Look as far as you can see in every direction—north and south, east and west. I am giving all this land, as far as you can see, to you and your descendants as a permanent possession. And I will give you so many descendants that, like the dust of the earth, they cannot be counted! Go and walk through the land in every direction, for I am giving it to you."
>
> —Genesis 13:14–17 NLT

God wants us to walk this way too. He wants us to view our surroundings with eyes of faith and take the land. He wants us to look at problems with faith-filled hearts and *see* them differently. He wants to expand our vision and believe for His plans here on Earth by faith and through faith. Faith empowers us. Because we are His children, we can look at people and circumstances with God's faith-filled perspective. We don't have to draw from just our own supply of faith either. We can actually draw from *God's* faith! Seeing with God's faith and believing for the changes He wants is the underlying premise of this book. What fantastic opportunities our lives in Christ grant us!

God wants us to live a lifestyle filled with His supernatural power. As Christ followers, we bear witness to His promises and walk in His truth so we may reach the world. This is the heart of our ministry. This book will give you hope, strength, and wisdom as you learn to walk in the supernatural today—and prepare for eternal life with Him later. This book contains the keys you need to fulfill your unique faith-filled mission here on Earth right here, right now.

CHAPTER 1

Experience the Supernatural Life

W E ARE BLESSED WITH God's *supernatural* power—today. We do not have to wait to get to heaven to experience the supernatural. The supernatural should be a central part of our lives every day. However, because of satan's constant interference in our spiritual growth, living in the *natural* world can be difficult. We often feel weary as we deal with troubles and fight temptation. We have to deal with tension, strife, crime, hatred, corruption, and the like just like everyone else. Nevertheless, the truth remains that we have access to the power and faith of God. He did not leave us dependent on our own strength and abilities. satan would love for us to live like that, but that's not

> ### *Supernatural*

part of God's plan at all. He gave us very real power. He wants us to live what I like to call "the high life" with Him.

> **And Jesus came and spake unto them, saying, All power is given unto me in heaven and in earth.**
>
> —Matthew 28:18

Faith is based on God's supernatural power. Without faith, we can't experience His power or please Him. Faith feeds on impossibility—it is opposite of human reason. And God wants us to *grow* in faith, not just stay where we are.

> **We are bound to thank God always for you, brethren, as it is meet, because that your faith groweth exceedingly, and the charity of every one of you all toward each other aboundeth.**
>
> —2 Thessalonians 1:3

God wants us to live our lives partnering with Him and in step with Him. He gave the earth to mankind and commanded us to be stewards over it. (A steward is one who takes care of some goods for another.) As a caretaker over the earth, nothing is supposed to happen here without our permission. That's where faith and vision come into play. How far can you see?

When Ezekiel looked into the valley and saw all those bones, He spoke to them and in time, life came back to them. You can do the same. You're going to speak to things, and the words and power that you're going to carry is going to bring forth something living. God's power will do that.

It's time to ask God to fill you with His faith so you can see the world around you as it ought to be. Then you can begin to declare His Word over it and release the Holy Spirit into every part that is out of line. God will faithfully execute His will.

As you persevere and fight the battle, keep your eyes on Christ, and learn to see everything through Him instead of listening to other people. God does not expect you to handle life dependent on human reason. He extends His wisdom and arsenal of faith to you instead.

What is faith? The Bible tells us this in simple terms:

> **Now faith is the substance of things hoped for, the evidence of things not seen.**
> —Hebrews 11:1

This means that no matter how impossible God's calling in your life might seem, you should trust Him, follow Him, and resist the temptation to make decisions based on logic alone. If God has called you, He has also provided the means to execute that calling. He is the God of the impossible. He is the God who wants us to walk on a higher path with Him. So what's the problem?

Logic Is of This World; Faith Is of the Supernatural World

As human beings, we naturally follow our own minds instead of going outside our comfort zones and accessing God's way. But human reason and logic aren't trustworthy. Never let what your reason tells you determine what your heart believes. Nowhere in the Bible did logic produce a miracle.

Most of the knowledge taught in our educational institutions is practical and logical. It makes sense, but human reason will always be on the opposite side of faith.

God wants us to live in the supernatural realm, in the high life.

The day God calls us home to be with Him eternally will be glorious. No longer will we have to endure the natural realm (and that will be wonderful), but we don't live passively looking ahead to heaven. No, we live actively declaring God's will through His Word by faith. As we grow, we learn to *see* the world through faith. Remember, we can

> *We live actively declaring God's will through His Word by faith.*

actually see with God's faith—all the time. So, living in the supernatural realm is not an *event*. It's a *lifestyle*—one we practice all the time.

> **For therein is the righteousness of God revealed from faith to faith: as it is written, The just shall live by faith.**
>
> —Romans 1:17

Since we live in the natural world for our entire lives, we tend to expect things to be logical, to make sense. Our comfort zone is in our human reason, and that's where the enemy wants us to stay. But we are to live by faith—the opposite of human reason—and we cannot understand God's ways through our human understanding. We are called to operate on a higher plane and live the high life. We are called to live by faith and see changes all around us brought about by faith.

When we abide in faith, miracles can happen. Miracles are for today. God performs miracles right here, every day. They are mysteries, but we can embrace those mysteries and walk in them. Mysteries make you masters. When you flow in mysteries, the supernatural realm is where you make your home. This is where we have been ordained to live and operate and do things on Earth, so let's embrace His signs and wonders.

> *Mysteries make you masters.*

> Behold, I and the children whom the Lord
> hath given me are for signs and for
> wonders in Israel from the Lord of hosts,
> which dwelleth in mount Zion.
>
> —Isaiah 8:18

We're here for signs and wonders! Don't forget that!

Don't Let People Fool You

As children of God, we must practice discernment. We must abide by God's teachings and commands, and resist the influences of the world.

> **Beware lest any man spoil you through
> philosophy and vain deceit, after the
> tradition of men, after the rudiments of the
> world, and not after Christ.**
>
> —Colossians 2:8

Sometimes when you read one translation of the Bible, you might not be sure about the meaning of a particular verse, so it's helpful to read many translations of the same Scripture. Here is that same verse from the Contemporary English Version:

> **Don't let anyone fool you by using senseless
> arguments. These arguments may sound
> wise, but they are only human teachings.
> They come from the powers of this world
> and not from Christ.**
>
> —Colossians 2:8 CEV

People can fool you, especially when the enemy is trying to make you stray from God's calling. People can be extremely persuasive, and we often feel compelled to follow their advice. However, if what they're saying does not line up with what you know about the Lord, walk away. Reject it. That's not of the kingdom of God. It's garbage.

God Almighty is saying that there is no comparison between worldly teachings and the teaching of Christ. God's teachings are perfect, while ours are flawed. No surprise there. Every argument, every tension, every unpleasant thing comes from the powers of this world. satan stirs up arguments and strife in an attempt to gain control of the message we hear. He wants to distract us so we lose our focus.

Therefore, we must not elevate the words and ways of this world so that they are more important than God's Word and direction in our lives. We must walk closely with Him so we can keep our focus on His ways. If we walk the high life, we will engage in activities that strengthen our faith, and expect the impossible. Remind yourself that the Word of God, the gospel, is not logical. Miracles are not logical. Eternal life is not logical. But they all are very real. God is alive.

Don't let people fool you. When you claim His promises, He faithfully answers.

He Is a God of Miracles

Some theologians claim that miracles are "apostolic," meaning they only happened when the first apostles were alive. They say that technology is responsible for all we accomplish today. But this is not true. It's just another device the enemy uses to distance us from our Creator. In fact, satan wants to take miracles out of the picture altogether. Even so, miracles are still happening every day all around us.

One definition of a *miracle* is "a phenomenal or supernatural event in the physical world that surpasses all known human or natural powers."

The Bible describes so many miracles that even the most educated biblical scholars cannot count them. Jesus healed and cast out demons from many people. Each one of those events was a miracle. He also turned water into wine, and He fed thousands of people with just two loaves of bread and five fish. He performed miracles everywhere He went.

Why did Jesus perform miracles? There are several reasons. Even when Jesus lived and ministered in the flesh, skeptics and naysayers refused to believe He was the Son of God. So Jesus performed miracles to reveal who He was. Additionally, Jesus performed miracles to glorify God the Father. Last of all, He wanted to give us a preview of what eternal life with Him would be like. Hallelujah! Jesus modeled a lifestyle of performing miracles when He was here, and God is still performing miracles today—through and for each of us. He has not changed.

A Miracle in This Ministry

God has helped our ministry accomplish miracles right here on Earth. Here's an example: In the late 1990s, God called us to start a business school as part of this ministry. In 1998, I said to two of our faithful members, "You've been through some of the country's finest MBA programs. You know a lot about businesses. Gather some information, and tell me how long it's going to take to start the business school that God has called us to launch."

They came back and said it would take one to two years.

I said, "Let me pray about that." I went home and prayed about it. God told me it would only take two months. And it did.

Within just two months, we established the Joseph Business School (JBS) in Forest Park, Illinois. Our mission is to equip entrepreneurs and individuals using practical and biblical principles to raise up companies and create wealth, and to transform desolate places into flourishing communities for the glory of God— in other words, to reach the world. The school is nationally accredited by ACCET (Accrediting Council for Continuing Education and Training), and it has a presence on five continents plus an online program!

That's not logical, is it?

Based on the standards of the natural world, it seems impossible. But again, faith is infinitely more powerful than logic.

Over and over again in my life, God told me to do something that defied human reason. I came to Chicago with two hundred dollars and no place to stay because God told me to do that. And He had a plan. We just have to listen with faith and do what God tells us. That's the high life that we are called to live.

Rise from the Low Life to the High Life

**Behold, I and the children whom the LORD
hath given me are for signs and for wonders**

**in Israel from the LORD of hosts, which
dwelleth in mount Zion.**

—Isaiah 8:18

If you belong to Christ—if you seek Him out—you will experience signs and wonders. A lot of times, we think we are going to fulfill our destinies without miracles, without signs, without wonders—without His supernatural intervention. But we cannot.

As long as we live in this world according to our human understanding, we are living the "low life." You rise to the high life when you put your faith in God and He gives you some direction. He will task you with a calling that might seem impossible, but faith is fed with the impossible. It's difficult for our human minds to believe in miracles—in the signs and wonders He sends us. We try to figure them out. We think about them at length, trying to make sense of them.

We must move the miracles, the possibilities, the signs, and the wonders out of our minds and claim them by faith. We must use the imaginations God gave us so we can see through faith. Faith partners us with God. He moves *only* by faith. And the only way we can please Him is through faith:

> **But without faith it is impossible to please
> him: for he that cometh to God must
> believe that he is, and that he is a rewarder
> of them that diligently seek him.**
>
> —Hebrews 11:6

You were born to live in faith, trusting in Him. He wants you to *see* far beyond what you can see with your physical eyes. God wants you to *see* with your imagination. He is not limited by distance or time. God wants you to appropriate His faith over every situation. He wants you to *see with His eyes* and speak His will into existence through faith.

Claim His miracles! He wants you to be excited when the impossible happens. Too often we continue to seek out logic in our lives instead of relying on faith. When we do this, we cannot see very far. Moses is a good example.

Moses Disobeys God

In Exodus, God called Moses to lead six million people (the Israelites) from slavery in the land of Egypt to the Promised Land. God promised them that they would make it there, but they faced challenges along the way.

At one point, the people became tired and thirsty. They asked for water, so Moses asked God what to do. God told Moses to strike a rock. Moses obeyed God, and water spewed forth!

Years later, the people became thirsty again and requested water. Again, Moses asked God what to do. This time, God told Moses to *speak* to the rock instead of *striking* the rock:

> Take the rod, and gather thou the assembly
> together, thou, and Aaron thy brother, and
> speak ye unto the rock before their eyes;
> and it shall give forth his water, and thou
> shalt bring forth to them water out of the
> rock: so thou shalt give the congregation
> and their beasts drink.
>
> —Numbers 20:8

But Moses disobeyed God and *struck* the rock instead of *speaking* to it. Water still came forth, but the end result was catastrophic—Moses was not allowed to enter the Promised Land.

> And Moses lifted up his hand, and with his
> rod he smote the rock twice: and the water
> came out abundantly, and the congregation

> drank, and their beasts also. And the LORD
> spake unto Moses and Aaron, Because ye
> believed me not, to sanctify me in the eyes
> of the children of Israel, therefore ye shall
> not bring this congregation into the land
> which I have given them.
>
> —Numbers 20:11–12

Now, why did Moses disobey God? Maybe he was angry. Maybe he was feeling rebellious. Maybe he thought for sure that God must mean for him to *strike* the rock because that is what He had told him to do before. We don't know, but Moses was relying on logic, not faith.

God punished Moses because He wanted to teach him to rely on faith in God and His commands, and God expects the same obedience from us. We must abide in Him and seek His guidance. Whether He tells us to strike or speak, we must do what He says. Moses was a great man, but he didn't listen.

God Created the Heavens and the Earth by Speaking

Through God's divine power, speaking is powerful. That's how He created the heavens and the earth.

> In the beginning God created the heaven and the earth. And the earth was without form, and void; and darkness was upon the face of the deep. And the Spirit of God moved upon the face of the waters. And God said, Let there be light: and there was light. And God saw the light, that it was good: and God divided the light from the darkness.
>
> —Genesis 1:1–4

In these very lines of the Bible, we see the supernatural way God created every living thing. He simply *spoke* to create each element of the heavens and the earth. If He can create simply by speaking, imagine what we can do through Him when we speak the miracles we need to see manifested in our lives. That's what faith does.

We can change a situation that seems beyond repair simply by seeing God's plan and speaking possibility and love into it. When our children are not acting right, we must discipline them, but we should also instill in them that we believe they will accomplish great things at the same time. We need to say, "Go to your room. You're going to be a lawyer. Go to your room. You will be the finest physician that's ever lived."

We need to go to jails and prisons and speak possibility into people's lives. We need to have vision for them. We need to tell them, "You're going to be a lawyer. You're going to be a doctor."

Jesus Heals Ten Lepers

The Bible is full of stories about Jesus performing miracles, often simply by speaking them. In Luke, there is an account of Jesus healing ten men all at once!

On His way from Jerusalem one day, Jesus came across ten lepers. They asked Him to take pity on them. Jesus told them, "Go, show yourselves to the priests." As they went, they were cleansed. One of the men, a Samaritan, came back to Jesus, praising God. He fell at Jesus' feet and thanked Him. Jesus asked why the other nine men had not come back to give thanks for their healing, and said this to the one man:

And he said unto him, Arise, go thy way:
thy faith hath made thee whole.

—Luke 17:19

Never underestimate the power of God. He is omnipotent, omnipresent, and omniscient.

Follow Him in Faith

God wants us to follow His every command and abide by faith. When we do that, we can see far beyond what we would otherwise be able to see. We can see with God's eyes. And we can believe in miracles.

I thought about this story about Jesus healing the lepers when the COVID-19 pandemic began to emerge in 2020. Like many churches, we had to cancel our in-person services.

One day, my secretary called me and said, "Pastor, you've got a healing service on the calendar here. Are you going to keep that, even though no one is able to come here?"

I thought about that for a second. God wants us to lay hands on sick people so they can be healed. He wants us to reach the world. I waited to hear from God. He said, "Yes, keep it."

I told her, "Yes, we're going to keep it."

God was telling me to speak to the obstacle we were facing, just like He told Moses to speak to the rock. No one was coming except a couple of people who were assisting me. This was a whole new paradigm. How was I going to have a healing meeting? Normally I could lay hands on them. Now I couldn't. I asked God what to do, and He reminded me of this:

> **The centurion answered and said, Lord, I am not worthy that thou shouldest come under my roof: but speak the word only, and my servant shall be healed.**
>
> —Matthew 8:8

He gave me greater vision. I didn't need people in the room. I just had to *speak* the word. God was challenging me to see farther, to believe that He could heal people without my laying hands on them. I knew He could do that. The question was: How far could I see? I had to speak and expect Him to move. I didn't get to see it right away either. I had to wait.

Did people get healed that day? Yes, they did! We got 633 messages from people who were healed in that meeting! 633! We must listen for the voice of God and then obey Him.

> **And it shall come to pass, if thou shalt**
> **hearken diligently unto the voice of the**
> **LORD thy God, to observe and to do all his**
> **commandments which I command thee**
> **this day, that the LORD thy God will set thee**
> **on high above all nations of the earth: and**
> **all these blessings shall come on thee, and**
> **overtake thee, if thou shalt hearken unto**
> **the voice of the LORD thy God.**
>
> —Deuteronomy 28:1–2

Now, how are these blessings guaranteed to come on you? We must hearken to His voice. We've got to hear God and then do what He tells us to do. When we do, His blessings will run us over.

It is time for God's children to stop living in fear and claim His miracles. To do that, we must walk closely with Him, listen to His voice, and obey His commands. We must see farther, replace logic with faith, and strive to achieve the impossible, through His strength and vision. We must see farther and enter the realm of impossibility so God's faith can be made manifest.

Miracles Confirm the Truth

The enemy hates the miracles our Lord performs. He tries to cancel out miracles, but he is no match for God. satan tries to take miracles out of the church, out of businesses, and out of our lives.

It is glorious that our God just keeps right on performing miracles anyway! His miracles confirm the truth that Jesus is alive. Just as in the days when Jesus walked the earth, His miracles work on skeptics and cause them to turn to Christ. Glory to God!

There was a time when I could not see very far. But once I learned to abide by faith and allow Him to lead me, I began to see infinite possibilities through Him.

CHAPTER 2

Know That Jesus *Is* the Word

In the beginning was the Word, and the Word was with God, and the Word was God.

—John 1:1

WHEN WE TALK ABOUT the Word of God, we are often referring to the Bible. But did you know that the Word *is* Jesus Himself too? That's right. Jesus Christ is not only our King, Lord, and Savior, but He is also the *Word of God*.

When Jesus lived on Earth, some followed Him, but many rejected Him. When He died on the cross for our sins, He fulfilled His task as the Lamb of God. He redeemed all of mankind. When He returns in the

Second Coming, He will perform a much different role as the Lion of the tribe of Judah. He will rise up against His enemies.

In Revelation, the apostle John painted the vision of Jesus' glorious return as He appears riding a white horse:

> And I saw heaven opened, and behold a white horse; and he that sat upon him was called Faithful and True, and in righteousness he doth judge and make war. His eyes were as a flame of fire, and on his head were many crowns; and he had a name written, that no man knew, but he himself. And he was clothed with a vesture dipped in blood: and his name is called The Word of God.
>
> —Revelation 19:11–13

The Word leads us to reach the world:

> But the righteousness which is of faith speaketh on this wise, Say not in thine heart, Who shall ascend into heaven? (that is, to bring Christ down from above:) Or, Who shall descend into the deep? (that is, to bring up Christ again from the dead.)

> **But what saith it? The word is nigh thee,**
> **even in thy mouth, and in thy heart: that is,**
> **the word of faith, which we preach.**
> —Romans 10:6–8

This means we shouldn't try to get Jesus to come up from the dead or come down from heaven. He's been here already. We must simply preach His truth so we can reach the world. The New International Version translates that last verse as follows:

> **"The word is near you; it is in your mouth**
> **and in your heart," that is, the message**
> **concerning faith that we proclaim.**
> —Romans 10:8 NIV

To make sure we reach the world with the message He wants us to preach, He— the Word—is in our mouths and hearts. We need to immerse ourselves in the Word and speak the Word daily.

The Word of God appeals to both our understanding and our *imaginations*. We need to apply our imaginations too. Some people seem to be afraid of their imaginations in the same way that one might be afraid to drive after an accident. We'll talk more about fear later, but suffice it to say that we need to allow God to use our minds and imaginations as we apply His Word to our lives.

When we are in step with the Word, Jesus creates miracles through action. But again, we must have faith and *believe* that Jesus can and will perform miracles to glorify the kingdom of God. We must believe in what we cannot see.

Think about this: If Jesus is the Word, then whatever Jesus could do, the Word can do.

> **Whatever Jesus could do, the Word can do.**

The reason some people say the Word has done nothing for them is because they don't believe the Word. This is why it is critical for us, as followers of Christ, to meditate on Him, study the Bible, pray earnestly, seek Him, and follow His commands. These efforts to get closer to Him will transform us and lead us into the high life God wants for us.

We will see a situation in life and think, *If Jesus were here right now, He would* _____. Then we can speak the Word and see a miracle happen because whatever Jesus could do, the Word can still do today.

That's amazing! Think of how Jesus wants to transform the people and situations in your life. Use the Word!

We should have miracles operating in our lives. Miracles follow laws. They are a natural response to speaking the Word of God by faith.

The gospel was never meant to be preached without signs and wonders, so we must get from simply preaching to preaching and seeing miracles. That's real Holy Spirit preaching! We should see miracles everywhere we go. We should expect God to answer us.

Since the Word of God never returns void as it says in Isaiah 55:11, we can live expectantly and allow the Word to expand our vision using our imaginations with eyes of faith. Remember, our imaginations are not evil. They are a gift from God. Our imaginations are creative and are meant to be used in partnership with God's Word and faith.

The Word releases the Holy Spirit into any place we declare it, as we hear from God. This is why meditation and communication with God are so important. If we hear from Him and declare what He is saying through

His Word, it will come to pass. If it's just out of our own brains, it won't.

Remember what Jesus said about us though:

> **My sheep hear my voice, and I know them,**
> **and they follow me.**
>
> —John 10:27

We have the capacity to hear His voice. We can take any problem or question to Him and He will direct us. And we can see Him changing the world around us, putting it in alignment with His Word. Get excited!

Jesus, as the Word of God, also saves us from destruction:

> **He sent his word, and healed them, and**
> **delivered them from their destructions.**
>
> —Psalm 107:20

Jesus delivers us from all our fears. God sent His Word (Jesus) to heal and deliver when the world was dominated by Rome. Jesus did both those things when He walked the earth, and He is still doing that today through all of us. Nothing can withstand the power of God's Word.

CHAPTER 3

Imitate Your Heavenly Father

And God said, Let us make man in our image, after our likeness.

-—Genesis 1:26

G OD CREATED EACH ONE of us in His own image. This means we have His nature. He wants us to imitate Him—to be like Him—in the way we think and act. He has planned out every moment of our lives carefully. He intends for us, His children, to hear Him, trust Him, and do what He directs us to do.

How Can We Imitate Him as Flawed Humans?

Now, when Adam and Eve fell in the Garden of Eden—eating the forbidden fruit—the human race became tainted and disfigured. When mankind did that, everything changed because the earth did not belong to God anymore. At that time, the Holy Spirit and the angels had to leave. After that, they came and ministered whenever God sent them, like when Jacob saw them in Genesis going up and down into heaven. However, they could no longer live here. Throughout the Old Testament, they came and helped God's servants. But God had a better plan in mind.

He sent Himself to be the perfect sacrifice so we could be redeemed and restored to relationship with Him. Jesus preached the good news and delivered and healed.

Some time after Jesus died, went to heaven, and put the blood on the altar—the mercy seat—the Holy Ghost came rushing down like a mighty wind. Now the Holy Spirit had permission to cover the earth again. So how does this work now?

When we are born again, the Holy Spirit inhabits us and dwells in us. He works through us. Jesus said this:

> **Verily, verily, I say unto you, He that believeth on me, the works that I do shall he do also; and greater works than these shall he do; because I go unto my Father. And whatsoever ye shall ask in my name, that will I do, that the Father may be glorified in the Son. If ye shall ask any thing in my name, I will do it.**
>
> —John 14:12–14

Today we get to partner with God in His work in the earth. Now that the Holy Spirit is here, we have the authority to speak and release Him to heal and act. We don't do the healing or take the action. He does that, but we are part of the process. God set it up this way.

God loves us. He tells us so in Ephesians 5:1. This partnership is His plan.

> **Be ye therefore followers of God, as dear children.**
>
> —Ephesians 5:1

The Amplified Bible translates it this way:

> **Therefore become imitators of God [copy**
> **Him and follow His example], as well-**
> **beloved children [imitate their father].**
> —Ephesians 5:1 AMP

The example used above is of beloved children imitating their father. That's just not good reading or wise advice—it is a *command*. He is our Father, and we are His children. He wants us to follow Him closely and live our lives in the supernatural. He wants us to do what He is doing just as Jesus did.

> **Then answered Jesus and said unto them,**
> **Verily, verily, I say unto you, The Son can**
> **do nothing of himself, but what he seeth the**
> **Father do: for what things soever he doeth,**
> **these also doeth the Son likewise.**
> —John 5:19

How can we even begin to imitate Him when we are flawed humans and He is the perfect divine Father? Through the indwelling of His Holy Spirit, that's how. Through the Holy Spirit, we can be holy and set apart to do His work.

> **But as he which hath called you is holy, so**
> **be ye holy in all manner of conversation;**

because it is written, Be ye holy; for I am holy.

—1 Peter 1:15–16

Be ye therefore perfect, even as your Father which is in heaven is perfect.

—Matthew 5:48

That isn't logical, is it? How can we be perfect like Him when we are basically flawed? Remember, it's not logical. We cannot understand His ways with our own human understanding. It's beyond what our minds can comprehend.

We must try to see farther, to see beyond the facts before us. We must see with the eyes of the Spirit. We can only follow God and be like Him through the working of the Holy Spirit within us. He transforms us from the inside out. He opens our eyes.

> *We need to see as far as our eyes can see with eyes of faith.*

We need to see *as far as our eyes can see* with eyes of faith.

So how far can you see? Consider this concept in every situation you encounter. One of the central themes of the Bible is the transforming power of God and the way He changes us to be more like Him. As we are transformed by God, we will also transform the world around us as He desires. He sends us to speak the Word of God over situations that are out of order. His power will transform them just as His Spirit is transforming us. Wow!

CHAPTER 4

Believe That God Will Cancel Your Debts

**And you, being dead in your sins and
the uncircumcision of your flesh, hath
he quickened together with him, having
forgiven you all trespasses; blotting out the
handwriting of ordinances that was against
us, which was contrary to us, and took it
out of the way, nailing it to his cross.**

—Colossians 2:13–14

TODAY—MORE THAN EVER, IT seems—we are faced with challenges and the stress of a fast-paced life. Sometimes, we are so busy trying to keep up with our family, career, financial, and other responsibilities that we lose sight of God's promises to us.

When we become followers of Christ, children of the Living God, our challenges do not cease. They do not go away. This is one of the many reasons we need to live the high life with God.

As long as we are living in this world and abiding by its ways, we are not a threat to satan. But once we are born again and live with Jesus as our Savior and Lord, everything changes. We begin to follow His ways, intentionally shunning the ways of the natural world and choosing to live in the supernatural realm with Him instead. Then we become a huge threat to satan.

So what does he do? He works on you. He tempts you. He tries to make you stray from God's ways. Because we are human, each one of us sins. We make bad choices. Sometimes, we have self-doubt. We experience distress, sadness, anger, jealousy, and on and on.

satan uses those negative feelings against us. He uses sin to make us doubt that God would want us as His children. We know we owed a debt we could never pay, and satan reminds us of that.

But today is a glorious day! Why? Because today is the day of unprecedented cancellations!

As promised in the verse from Colossians quoted earlier and in other references in the Bible, God will *cancel the debt* with which the enemy has bound you. Your debt of sin—all of it—has been canceled by the blood of Jesus Christ.

Today is your day of liberation from the sin that has kept you bound. The Spirit of God is untying those shackles and chains. He wants us to be free so we can be the strongest possible messengers for His glory. The Living God needs you, me—each one of His children. He needs every son and every daughter:

> **And it shall come to pass in the last days,**
> **saith God, I will pour out of my Spirit upon**
> **all flesh: and your sons and your daughters**
> **shall prophesy, and your young men shall**
> **see visions, and your old men shall dream**
> **dreams.**
>
> —Acts 2:17

And He doesn't stop there. God wants us to be free from anything that binds us from walking in Him and reaching our purpose.

If we can speak and people get saved, why can't we speak and get debts canceled?

We can! We must believe it and claim it. God wants us to live the high life with Him. That means we cannot be financially crippled either. We can speak to those debts, and He will help us be free of them so we can walk a faith-filled life. (More on that later.)

Prepare yourself for this turnaround, this change. Look, see, and gather what the Lord has in store for you in every facet of your life. Gather what belongs to you, for there is much that belongs to you!

His Ways Are Higher than Our Ways

God created the universe and everything in it, including each one of us. He plans everything with purpose—He does nothing randomly. He created each one of us to fulfill a specific purpose. In our own human understanding, we cannot understand all His reasons. His ways are higher than our ways, as we learn in Isaiah:

> For my thoughts are not your thoughts,
> neither are your ways my ways, saith the
> LORD. For as the heavens are higher than
> the earth, so are my ways higher than your
> ways, and my thoughts than your thoughts.
> For as the rain cometh down, and the snow

> from heaven, and returneth not thither,
> but watereth the earth, and maketh it bring
> forth and bud, that it may give seed to the
> sower, and bread to the eater: so shall my
> word be that goeth forth out of my mouth:
> it shall not return unto me void, but it shall
> accomplish that which I please, and it shall
> prosper in the thing whereto I sent it.
>
> —Isaiah 55:8–11

That is a powerful set of verses. We're talking about the Word of God here. This is saying that wherever the Word goes, it

The Word has miracle action.

will prosper. That means the Word has *miracle action*. Words come with miracle action!

We just learned about imitating our Father, the Creator and Master of the universe. Since He is a Creator, He expects us to create things too. He expects us to use His Word and walk in His creative power to bring forth His fruit.

This might be a business school, as it has been for me. It can be anything that He has planned to prosper you. His ideas are as unique and different as we are.

The important thing is to hear from Him and begin to go in the direction He sends you.

God's righteousness will be revealed soon! When you declare Him as Lord, you will be led out in joy and led forth in peace. Now go in the name of Jesus Christ, and declare that He is Lord. Declare this glorious truth, and you will see the greatness of God upon you.

He Wants Us to Thrive Financially

Temptation to sin is just one of the ways satan tries to separate us from God. He uses many devices, and one of them is debt—financial stress. As long as we are worried about paying our bills and providing for our families, we cannot claim God's promises and miracles.

> *Redemption is not complete without divine provision.*

God does not want you to toil your life away trying to pay debts. Your full redemption includes your financial salvation, so paying off a debt is part of it. You are redeemed from debt, from lack, from fruitlessness. Take advantage of your redemptive rights.

God never intended for you to be broke. Redemption is not complete without divine provision. It is unjust for you to get saved and be broke.

When I was working at IBM, I had a mountain of debt. Then I was born again. One day, I heard a man in the congregation talk about his debts. He said he would pay what he could, but he couldn't pay everyone. Every month he paid what he could and got angry letters from those he wasn't able to pay.

Then one day, he laid all his bills on the kitchen table. He spread them out and spoke to those debts. Soon, he paid off all his debt.

When I heard his story, I thought, "If Jesus will do that for him, He will do it for me. It just depends on how far I can see." Could I see those debts canceled?

So I put all my bills on the table and spoke to them, saying, "Debt, I command you to dematerialize. Disappear. Go away. Be canceled. Be paid off in Jesus' name."

Within one year, I was completely out of debt. Remember, God can do what's impossible for us to do in our own human strength and understanding. We must believe that He will and He can.

So if you are financially stressed, you are not bound. There is not a problem that is too big for God. He's not leaving you on your own in it. Debt does not have to prevent you from serving God. He wants you free of it and free indeed! He wants to cancel that debt.

Please read the following out loud, believing God will do this: Right now, I speak to every debt I owe. I command my debt to be supernaturally paid off, to disappear in the name of Jesus. It is *done* in Jesus' name! Amen.

Now give God praise for His love and mercy.

CHAPTER 5

Live from the Inside Out

ONE OF THE BOOKS I wrote, *The Kingdom of God in You*, focused on living from the inside out. The revised version was published in 2021.

In the book, I explained how to escape the prison of the enemy's deception and how to experience God's kingdom power. I described the power for daily living that you can experience when you rely on Him instead of relying on your own personal effort.

When I first got into ministry years ago, I had the following Scripture printed on all my business cards:

> **And my speech and my preaching was**
> **not with enticing words of man's wisdom,**
> **but in demonstration of the Spirit and of**
> **power: that your faith should not stand in**

> the wisdom of men, but in the power of
> God.
>
> —1 Corinthians 2:4–5

And it's the truth! Beloved, our faith should not stand in the wisdom of men but in the power of God.

Be *In* Control, Not *Under* Control

So what does it mean to live from the inside out?

Well, it's the reverse of the way we naturally do things. As flawed humans, we tend to live from the outside in. This means we let the outside world influence us. When we do that, we are *under* its control. Countless distractions, assaults from the enemy, hardships, obstacles, and temptations prevent us from focusing on His kingdom. When we spend all our time and energy fighting battles in the natural world, we lose sight of His plan for us. We do not live each day operating in the supernatural with Him.

> *Beloved, our faith should not stand in the wisdom of men but in the power of God.*

When we live from the inside out, it means we are *in* control. We know, acknowledge, and understand what it means to be children of God, reaching the world to glorify Him. We make conscious choices to be like Him, imitate Him, and honor Him with our thoughts and actions.

We want to be *in* control, through God, not *under* the control of outside forces.

Speak Only about What You *Want* to Happen

When I started a little church in Minnesota, the daughter of one of the members got sick and went to the hospital. The girl's mom kept calling me, saying, "Pastor, come quick! Our daughter's sick, and all her systems are shutting down."

I said, "OK, I'll be there shortly."

I was busy at the time, so before I left, I finished mowing my lawn.

Now, when you first read that, you might think: *The girl was dying! Why didn't you rush to the hospital? Why did you finish mowing your lawn?*

Anyone who knows me knows I care deeply about every person in our ministry. I did not feel the need to rush because I knew God was in control of the situation. When you live from the inside out, you know God has everything under control.

After I finished mowing, I took a shower, ate a little food, and drove to the hospital. When I got there, the girl's mother ran down the hall toward me. She said, "I'm glad you're here! She's in intensive care."

Her daughter's skin had turned purple because her systems weren't working. I told her, "Put your hand on that side of her head, and I'll put my hand on this side." Then I said, "I'm going to pray."

The mom began to cry. "That's not going to help us! I appreciate it, but that won't help us at all." The mom was living from the outside in. She was letting her limited human knowledge and sight influence her. Her emotions took over. She was not *in* control; she was *under* control.

> *She quickly came to herself and began to pray with me in faith for her daughter, shifting the atmosphere from panic and fear to faith and confidence. God worked a miracle and her daughter fully recovered.*

She quickly came to herself and began to pray with me *in faith* for her daughter, shifting the atmosphere from panic and fear to faith and confidence. God worked a miracle and her daughter fully recovered.

See, we've got to live from the inside out. We can't let our emotions rule us. We've got to rule our emotions. This is an important lesson for every believer. We must rely on God, trust Him, and believe that He can—and will—intervene on our behalf.

Living from the inside out also means speaking only about what you *want* to happen. That girl's mom was letting her worries and fear take over. She was imagining the worst possible outcome for her daughter. That is not faith. Speak only in terms of what you *want* to happen.

> *Living from the inside out also means speaking only about what you want to happen.*

Expand Your Vision

Living from the inside out will also expand your vision. It is a purposeful, intentional, supernatural way of life. This is how you remain contented in the Spirit and peaceful, while purposefully establishing the kingdom of God in your life. Doing this is vital to building your faith.

Once again we come back to the question: How far can you see?

Your vision depends on your reliance on God too. When you know that you know that you know that He is in control, you will not be pushed around by anything. You will be secure in His love for you and His plan for your life.

No matter what happens, you will trust Him. As you do this, He will continue to encourage you by building your faith and your ability to see as He sees. He will use you to extend His kingdom even more.

CHAPTER 6

Call on God to Relieve Your Fears

Fear thou not; for I am with thee: be not dismayed; for I am thy God: I will strengthen thee; yea, I will help thee; yea, I will uphold thee with the right hand of my righteousness.

—Isaiah 41:10

SOMETIMES FEAR CAN CONSUME us. That's not surprising. We are surrounded by it.

We are afraid of getting sick, afraid of losing a job or home, afraid of flying, afraid of getting married again, afraid of being a parent, afraid our kids will stray from the teachings of the Lord. There is plenty to fear in this world—but God does not want fear to overwhelm us.

if we call on God, He will not only protect us, but He will also teach us to walk with good courage.

God Protected David from Saul's Vengeance

When we rely only on our human strength and understanding, we are vulnerable to attacks from the enemy. But when we believe God will deliver us, He will. One of the stories in the Bible that teaches this lesson well is about David in the Old Testament in 1 Samuel 17.

At the time, there was a war in the land of Israel. King Saul and the Israelite army were fighting the Philistines. One of the Philistines was a fierce giant named Goliath. David's brothers were in the Israelite army, and even the soldiers were afraid of Goliath.

David said he would kill Goliath, but of course no one believed him. How could a normal-sized young man possibly defeat a giant who was protected with a brass helmet, a shield, and heavy armor? Goliath had a spear the size of a small tree. What was this young shepherd against such a monster?

But David knew God would help him. Defeating Goliath would have been impossible for David if he relied on his human strength alone, but David declared that Goliath's size and armor were no match for the Lord:

> Then said David to the Philistine, Thou comest to me with a sword, and with a spear, and with a shield: but I come to thee in the name of the LORD of hosts, the God of the armies of Israel, whom thou hast defied.
>
> —1 Samuel 17:45

David loaded one smooth stone into his slingshot and shot it at Goliath's head, and it knocked Goliath right out. Then David cut off Goliath's head with Goliath's own sword. When the Philistines saw David kill Goliath, they became afraid and ran away.

> *David declared that Goliath's size and armor were no match for the Lord.*

After this victory, it would seem like David would be full of courage and without fear. But David still experienced paralyzing fear. Why? Because, as we learn in 1 Samuel 19, King Saul turned on David later and set out to kill him with his huge army! Saul was jealous of David's rising popularity and favor.

As Saul pursued David, David escaped repeatedly. During that continued cat-and-mouse game, God offered David much encouragement. God even used Israel's enemies to make it possible for David to escape.

Finally, David trapped Saul in a cave. He could have killed him easily but did not. Once Saul realized that David had spared his life, he was filled with remorse.

> **And he said to David, Thou art more righteous than I: for thou hast rewarded me good, whereas I have rewarded thee evil. And thou hast shewed this day how that thou hast dealt well with me: forasmuch as when the LORD had delivered me into thine hand, thou killedst me not. For if a man find his enemy, will he let him go well away? wherefore the LORD reward thee good for that thou hast done unto me this day. And now, behold, I know well that thou shalt surely be king, and that the kingdom of Israel shall be established in thine hand.**
>
> **—1 Samuel 24:17–20**

How did David deal with his fear? He called out to God to calm his fears:

> I sought the LORD, and he heard me, and
> delivered me from all my fears.
>
> —Psalm 34:4

Replace Fear with Faith

Fear is a deadly enemy. It is at the root of many poor choices. It can prevent us from doing as we ought to do. Fear can have a paralyzing effect on us. How many times have you heard people say they can't do something because they are afraid?

So fear is a common problem for us, but it's not one we have to allow. We can do what David did too. We can ask God to calm our fears.

Beyond that, fear prevents us from claiming God's miracles in our lives. We should expect miracles in business, in politics, in the classroom, at home, and in our relationships. Those miracles are life.

> My son, attend to my words; incline thine
> ear unto my sayings. Let them not depart
> from thine eyes; keep them in the midst
> of thine heart. For they are life unto those

that find them, and health to all their flesh. Keep thy heart with all diligence; for out of it are the issues of life.

—Proverbs 4:20–23

When we claim God's miracles, there is no room for fear.

> *When we claim God's miracles, there is no room for fear.*

Remember when Mary found out that she, a virgin, was to bear the Son of God? She was afraid! Such a thing was not logical. It did not make sense. In fact, it was impossible. And what would happen to her reputation—an unmarried woman having a child?

But Mary chose to trust God instead of giving in to fear. She believed what the angel told her and accepted the very difficult calling God had given her.

Again, you are designed in His image for the impossible. Faith is designed for the impossible, and it feeds on the impossible. God has given you the spirit of love, not fear. So resist fear, and ask God for His help. He delights in you and will help you live with good courage instead of fear.

Conclusion

ELOVED, WE DON'T NEED to tear down another statue. We're going to *own the land* on which the statue stands. We must think big because we are claiming our own promised land. We are meant to live in the supernatural world.

So how far can you see?

We must claim His miracles every day in every situation. We must see beyond our limited human vision. We must see with His eyes and let Him extend our vision into the supernatural realm.

You can be a millionaire, a billionaire, a leader, an influential person. As long as you keep your eyes on the prize—the *dunamis* power of God—and obey His commands, He will help you go deeper and accomplish more than you could ever do on your own.

When that happens, you will be a living witness for others who are shackled by the influences of this world. You will reach the world with your own story of

God's love, grace, forgiveness, and power. That is God's will for each and every one of us.

Let God use your imagination to see as far as your eyes can see by faith. May He bless you richly.

What about You?

1. Think of a time in your life when you sensed that God wanted you to take a specific action, even though it didn't seem logical, and you did it. You followed His guidance instead of human reason. What happened as a result of your obedience? How did this experience grow your faith and increase your vision?

2. God gave us His Word and His Spirit to guide us. Share an experience when you increased your vision through hearing from God and meditating on His Word.

3. How does the Word of God challenge your imagination to see with God's faith?

4. Think about *seeing* with faith. Choose an area in which you need to grow or wish to see a change. How far can you *see* for that change? Commit it to prayer and begin to speak forth what God gives you daily.

5. As Colossians 2:12–13 (NIV) tells us, Jesus "canceled the charge of our legal indebtedness, which stood against us and condemned us; he has taken it away, nailing it to the cross." What types of debts—financial or otherwise—are holding you back from experiencing the liberation of having your debts canceled? Identify them, pray on them, and turn them over to God. Say this prayer: "In the name of Jesus, I receive the debt-free anointing on my life today. What has been spoken has been done in Jesus' name. Amen." And then praise Him!

6. In what ways do you think you have been *under* the control of worldly influences? What would it take to live your life being *in* control through God's guidance instead? What practical, daily steps can you take to begin living from the inside out today?

7. Do you sometimes focus on what you don't want instead of what you do want? Intentionally change that by focusing and speaking what you want to see manifested in your life.

Prayer of Salvation

GOD LOVES YOU—NO MATTER who you are, no matter what your past. God loves you so much that He gave His one and only begotten Son for you. The Bible tells us that "…whoever believes in Him shall not perish but have eternal life" (John 3:16 NIV). Jesus laid down His life and rose again so that we could spend eternity with Him in heaven and experience His absolute best on Earth. If you would like to receive Jesus into your life, say the following prayer out loud and mean it from your heart.

Heavenly Father, I come to You admitting that I am a sinner. Right now, I choose to turn away from sin, and I ask You to cleanse me of all unrighteousness. I believe that Your Son, Jesus, died on the cross to take away my sins. I also believe that He rose again from the dead so that I might be forgiven of my sins and made righteous through faith in Him. I call upon the name of Jesus Christ to be the Savior and Lord of my life. Jesus, I choose to follow You and ask that You fill me with the power of the Holy Spirit. I declare that right now I am a child of God. I am free from sin and full of the righteousness of God. I am saved in Jesus' name. Amen.

If you prayed this prayer to receive Jesus Christ as your Savior for the first time, please contact us on the Web at www.billwinston.org to receive a free book.

William (Bill) Samuel Winston

B ILL WINSTON IS THE visionary founder and senior pastor of **Living Word Christian Center** in Forest Park, Illinois.

He is also founder and president of **Bill Winston Ministries**, a partnership-based global outreach ministry that shares the gospel through television, radio, and the internet; the nationally accredited **Joseph Business School** which has partnership locations on five continents and an online program; the **Living Word School of Ministry and Missions**; and **Faith Ministries Alliance (FMA)**, an organization of more than

800 churches and ministries under his spiritual covering in the United States and other countries.

The ministry owns and operates two shopping malls, **Forest Park Plaza** in Forest Park and **Washington Plaza** in Tuskegee, Alabama.

Bill is married to Veronica and is the father of three, Melody, Allegra, and David, and the grandfather of eight.

Books by Bill Winston

- *The Kingdom of God in You: Releasing the Kingdom, Replenishing the Earth, Revised and Updated*
- *The Law of Confession: Revolutionize Your Life and Rewrite Your Future with the Power of Words*
- *The Missing Link of Meditation*
- *The Power of Grace*
- *The Power of the Tithe*
- *The Spirit of Leadership: Leadership Lessons Learned from the Life of Joseph*
- *Training for Reigning: Releasing the Power of Your Potential*
- *Transform Your Thinking, Transform Your Life: Radically Change Your Thoughts, Your World, and Your Destiny*
- *Vengeance of the Lord: The Justice System of God*

Some books are available in other languages.

Connect with Us!

Connect with Bill Winston Ministries on social media.

Visit www.billwinston.org/social to connect with all of our official social media channels.

Bill Winston Ministries

P.O. Box 947

Oak Park, Illinois 60303-0947

(708) 697-5100

(800) 711-9327

www.billwinston.org

Bill Winston Ministries Africa

22 Salisbury Road

Morningside, Durban, KWA Zulu Natal 4001

+27(0)313032541

orders@billwinston.org.za www.billwinston.org.za

Bill Winston Ministries Canada

P.O. Box 2900 Vancouver BC V6B 0L4

(844) 298-2900

www.billwinston.ca

Prayer Call Center

(877) 543-9443